LAUGHTER IN THE SHADOW OF THE TREES

and Other Plays

BY JAMES PRIDEAUX

★

★

DRAMATISTS
PLAY SERVICE
INC.

These plays are dedicated to
Dame Wendy Hiller
with respect, admiration, and love

AUTHOR'S NOTE

No sets are required for any of these plays. LAUGHTER IN THE SHADOW OF THE TREES can be done with merely three lawn chairs and a rustic garden table.

THE LIBRARIAN requires a straight, hospital-type chair and a side table — nothing more.

ABRAHAM LINCOLN DIES AT VERSAILLES needs only a park bench.

ELEPHANTS can be performed with neither scenery nor furniture.

REQUIEM FOR US is best done on an absolutely bare stage.

If wished, projections may, of course, be used to enhance the mood. For ABRAHAM LINCOLN a formal garden might be projected, and for LAUGHTER a projection of leafy trees would serve. ELEPHANTS might have anything suggesting ancient Rome: columns, crumbling statuary, etc. Anything white and sterile would do for THE LIBRARIAN, with the possibility of a window outlined upstage. REQUIEM FOR US is best done on an empty stage with no hint of time or place.

CONTENTS

Laughter in the Shadow of the Trees

5) Marriage

Distinguished critic, slipping into state of dementia, cared for by supportive wife

1m 2w 1 setting

LAUGHTER IN THE SHADOW OF THE TREES was produced by BBC-World Service Drama (Gordon House, Producer) in London, England, in February, 1995. It was directed by John Theocharis. The cast was as follows:

MARTIN FARNSWORTH .... Sir John Gielgud
FELICIA FARNSWORTH .... Dame Wendy Hiller
JAN FARNSWORTH .... Elizabeth Bell

Laughter in the Shadow of the Trees

As the curtain rises a woman of, perhaps, 35 stands against the darkened stage and addresses the audience. As she speaks, a projection of the leaves of trees gradually appears on the rear of the stage. The lights are still not at full when she finishes and we see, only dimly, two figures behind her. One, the man, is seated in a twig chair. The other, a woman, stands beside him. The woman who is speaking is named Jan.

JAN. *(To audience.)* Many years ago my mother remarked at the dinner table that she wished to live like the people she saw in old photographs. They smiled, she said, and swung tennis rackets and went on picnics and made funny faces at the camera. People in old photographs, she said, were happy. They never seemed to be looking into the future at darkness and death. We children sat silently, unable to comprehend this curious observation. My father, as he had a habit of doing, brushed it aside with his hand. But now, these many years later, when I wish to see my mother, I can see her only in an aging photograph, her and my father. They are at the edge of our lawn, under the trees, out by the stone barbecue my father proudly built with his own hands. They are hugging one another and laughing. My mother is looking directly into the camera. And I feel that she was wiser than we knew. *(The lights come up to full as she exits. We now see a very handsome woman in her late sixties. She wears an expensive silk dress with a diamond brooch at the neck. She is "dressed up." Her name is Felicia Cartwright Farnsworth. Her husband, Martin Farnsworth, sits in the chair, a shawl over his shoulders. He is the same age, but seems older and the blankness in his eyes tells us that the mind is almost, if not entirely, gone. Where she is wonderfully cheerful, he is irascible. He is not without strength, however, and his mind may experience moments of astonishing clarity.)*

FELICIA. You do remember. You do remember, Martin. You couldn't have forgotten. You made it yourself. Carried the stone. Slapped on the cement. Created it before our very eyes. So physical. Such a physical thing to do. So unlike you. I burst with pride. We always used to eat out here. Don't you remember? When the weather was clement? Always. And the charcoal. And that stuff you used to squirt on it. Remember? Flames as high as your head. Like Dante's inferno. Or nothing, of course. Sometimes nothing. Nothing at all. No matter what you did. Not a flame. Oh, how annoying. I don't blame you for being annoyed. So annoying not getting the damn thing going. I don't blame you. Isn't it lovely today? Are you enjoying the day, Martin? Darling, are you enjoying the day? Not many more of these left, I shouldn't think. Felt a chill last night. Did you? The first chill. Autumn. So beautiful, but we know where it leads, don't we! No good can come of it. Oh, I do hate driving on ice.

MARTIN. What?

FELICIA. I said I do hate driving on ice, don't you?

MARTIN. Time?

FELICIA. Oh, good, darling, I knew you were with us. *(Consults watch.)* Now it's just a little before twelve. She should be here any minute. I've made a lovely salad. Do you think we should eat out here? Insects, I suppose. Do you want more spray? Martin, do you want more spray?

MARTIN. Time?

FELICIA. No, the verandah, I think. Better really. I do like it out here, though. Hmmm, smell the air! Oh, look how high the grass is! I hope he comes to mow soon. I ran into his mother at the supermarket and she said his head's full of going off to college, but he'll come one more time. I don't know what we'll do after that.

MARTIN. Uuhh?

FELICIA. It's the boy who mows, Martin.

MARTIN. Oooh.

FELICIA. Yes, he's going off to college. Isn't that astonishing? He was such a little thing when he first came to us, remember? I was afraid he couldn't even handle the mower. And now off to college. He says you're an inspiration to him. Now doesn't that make you proud? You're an inspiration to the young. Pleased me, I must say. Not to be forgotten. Still read. Lovely.

MARTIN. But it troubled me to pass Come Farme, where about 21 people have died of the plague — and three or four days since I saw a dead corpse in a coffin lie in the close unburied — and a watch is constantly kept there, night and day, to keep the people in — the plague making us as cruel as dogs one to another.

FELICIA. She'll be late if she doesn't get here soon.

MARTIN. Did you hear what I said?

FELICIA. Yes, dear. The plague. 1665.

MARTIN. The plague making us as cruel as dogs one to another.

FELICIA. Like AIDS, isn't it, dear? Same thing. Oh, how astute of you to see it. Nothing changes. Certainly not human nature. I'm getting a little anxious, I really am. She's not a very good driver, really.

MARTIN. You're a foolish woman.

FELICIA. And she drinks, of course. Oh, but not this early surely. Not before lunch. I thought I'd serve a little sherry. Would you like a little sherry, Martin?

MARTIN. You're not bright.

FELICIA. But we've got along, haven't we? All these years? Got along? Loved each other. A wonderful life, really. Success, books, money. Not to mention lovely children, really lovely. Marvelous the way they turned out. Jan's very happy with this new man, darling. They've got a nice roomy place in town. Facing south. Sun pouring in. Oh, very happy, she and Michael.

MARTIN. Who is this Michael you keep harping on?

FELICIA. You met him. You remember. Rather heavy set, but terribly nice. Not a mean bone in his body. You remember, the one who can't seem to keep a job. There's a real sense of movement to his life.

MARTIN. The plague making us as cruel as dogs one to another.

FELICIA. I might as well confess I don't have any chocolate sauce. I do have ice cream, but I don't have any chocolate sauce. Is that a cloud? Oh, I hope it isn't going to rain.

MARTIN. I want chocolate sauce.

FELICIA. I know you do and I'm terribly sorry. I just forgot.

MARTIN. *(Starts to cry.)* I want chocolate sauce!

FELICIA. I'm sorry, darling, I'm really sorry. Now, don't cry. Jan's coming to see you. There's no need to cry. Think about the plague.

MARTIN. The plague making us as cruel as dogs one to another.

FELICIA. That's right. Terrible times. London decimated. I have a cold soup, too, so that'll be nice. Yes, everything's going to be lovely. Did I hear a car? *(Calls.)* Jan?

MARTIN. What are you doing?

FELICIA. I think she's here!

JAN. *(Calls from offstage.)* Mother?

FELICIA. *(Calls.)* We're out here, darling! At the back! *(To Martin.)* Yes, it *is* Jan. She's driven all the way from town just to see you. Your children do adore you, Martin, you might as well — *(Jan appears, carrying a bottle in a brown paper bag. She looks younger than she did when we first saw her.)*

JAN. What are you doing out here?

FELICIA. Well, I thought some air would do him good. Hello, my darling.

JAN. Hello, Mum. *(They embrace warmly.)* Hmmm, you look lovely. Hello, Daddy.

MARTIN. Who's this? *(Jan kisses him on the cheek, although he isn't entirely happy about it.)*

FELICIA. It's Jan, dear, come all the way from town just to —

MARTIN. *(Angrily to Felicia.)* Why do you do that?

FELICIA. Do what, Martin?

MARTIN. *(Mimics Felicia sourly.)* Do what, Martin?

FELICIA. I was just saying it's Jan.

MARTIN. Jan. Born October 4th, 1962. Weight 6 and three-quarter pounds. What more do you want?

FELICIA. Well, isn't that wonderful? I couldn't have remembered that.

MARTIN. *(Rises.)* I have to go to the bathroom.

FELICIA. Yes, all right, dear.

MARTIN. *(To Jan.)* I have to go to the bathroom, Jan.

FELICIA. Well, you don't have to announce it, dear. *(Takes Martin's arm.)* Let me help you. *(He suddenly gives her hand three sharp little slaps.)*

MARTIN. No, no, no! *(Felicia lets go of his arm.)* Help yourself, if you want to help somebody. Are you in the habit of following men to the bathroom?

FELICIA. No, frankly, I'm not.

MARTIN. *(Moving offstage.)* Stay seated, everyone. I should hate to think I'm beyond the point of capability when it comes to bodily functions. Anyone can do it. Midgets can do it. Nuns do it. *(Very solemnly; no hint of music.)* Argentines without means do it. People say in Boston even beans do it. *(He is gone.)*

JAN. Will he be all right?

FELICIA. Oh, yes ... yes, yes, yes. How nice to see you, darling.

JAN. *(Hands Felicia bag.)* I brought you some vodka.

FELICIA. *(Takes it.)* How delicious! We do like our little nip. Now, let's sit a minute. *(There are three twig chairs and a small table.)* How's Michael? Such a nice man, Michael.

JAN. We're breaking up.

FELICIA. Oh, my dear! I am sorry. We like Michael.

JAN. Yes. *(There is a pause.)*

FELICIA. Well, don't tell me if you don't want to.

JAN. Simple. He says he doesn't love me anymore.

FELICIA. I see. Well, it's been my experience that if people say they don't love you anymore they probably don't love you anymore.

JAN. What am I going to do? He's moving out. It hurts so much.

FELICIA. I'm sorry, dear Jan. Truly sorry.

JAN. Isn't it awful when somebody stops loving you?

FELICIA. I suppose it must be.

JAN. Well, you should know.

FELICIA. How would I know? *(Calls.)* Martin? Are you all right? *(To Jan.)* I always get a bit anxious when he's quiet too long. I don't think he's died, but I do think he might have gone into a faint. As long as he's talking all's right with the world.

JAN. Have you thought about what you're going to do?

FELICIA. Do?

JAN. Can you get help?

FELICIA. I do have help. You know that. Mary comes in once a week. Does all the heavy cleaning.

JAN. I meant a nurse.

FELICIA. Why should we have a nurse?

JAN. Mother, you've got to think about yourself.

FELICIA. I don't see why.

JAN. Isn't he getting worse?

FELICIA. Yes, he is.

JAN. Then you have to ... *(Shrugs.)* ... think about the future.

FELICIA. If I were to think about the future I'd go stark, staring mad.

JAN. Then let us do it. Gary and Mark and me. We've talked it over. Let us —

FELICIA. No, dear. Thank you, but I won't have you touching my husband. I don't consider the world a very happy place and I can't honestly say at this moment that I'm very happy. But there is one great joy at the center of my world and that is the love of my husband.

JAN. I know. But, darling, he ... well, he treats you so badly now. I wonder if he even ...

FELICIA. Even ... what?

JAN. ... even loves you anymore.

FELICIA. *(Rises.)* If I were to think for one moment that Martin didn't love me, I can assure you I would not go on living. Now let's change the subject.

JAN. *(After a long moment; looks around.)* What did you plant this year?

FELICIA. Oh, nothing much. Didn't feel like it. Did you know they're bringing out a new edition of his criticism? And they want to do a set of the essays?

JAN. Yes, you said. It's wonderful.

FELICIA. Well, it's one of the finest minds of our times. I get calls every day from people wanting to interview him. I put them off, of course. Everyone knows, but we pretend. What they don't know, though, is that he will have sudden flashes of remarkable clarity. Shining through. Right to the point. The perfect summing up. Out of the darkness the old Martin. And what I cling to ... my hope ... my strength ... is that out of that darkness he will one day say the few little words that are all I need to keep going. Just to say that he ...

JAN. Mother, I ...

FELICIA. *(Calls.)* Is that you, Martin? *(Martin enters, goes to his chair.)*

MARTIN. Jan, how lovely to see you! Why didn't you tell me Jan was here? *(He kisses Jan.)*

JAN. Hello, daddy. Don't you look well!

MARTIN. What a treat! *(Indicates bag.)* What's this? What's this?

FELICIA. She brought us some vodka. Isn't that nice?

MARTIN. It certainly is. It'll help keep out the plague. *(To Jan, intimately.)* It troubled me to pass Come Farme, where about 21 people have died of the plague — and three or four days since I saw a dead corpse in a coffin lie in the close unburied — and a watch is constantly kept there, night and day, to keep the people in — the plague making us as cruel as dogs one to another.

FELICIA. Sit down, dear.

MARTIN. Don't nag at me! I do hate that! Do you have AIDS, Jan?

JAN. I hope not, father.

MARTIN. I hope not, too. *(Sits.)* Nursie here has AIDS, you know. She'll die soon. A blessing, really. And much easier for me. Much easier.

FELICIA. *(After a moment.)* Shall we have a sip of something?

I bought some sherry.
JAN. Why not the vodka?
MARTIN. Why not?
FELICIA. Why not? I'll get glasses.
JAN. Let me help.
FELICIA. No, no, no. You stay and entertain your father. Are you all right, Martin? *(Martin doesn't reply, instead is smiling at Jan. Felicia exits.)*
JAN. How are you feeling, Dad?
MARTIN. The streets mighty empty all the way now, even in London, which is a sad sight. And to Westminster Hall, where talking, hearing very sad stories from Mrs. Mumford among others, of Mrs. Mitchell's son's family ...
JAN. Daddy ...
MARTIN. ... and poor Will that used to sell us ale at the Halldoor — his wife and three children dead, all I think in a day.
JAN. Are you feeling better?
MARTIN. You're a cool customer.
JAN. No, I'm not. I wish I could talk to you.
MARTIN. I get so bored with that, that wish I could talk to you stuff. Try to stop you, you and that woman.
JAN. I hear they're going to bring out a new edition of your criticism.
MARTIN. I don't criticize.
JAN. Oh, yes, you do. Books ... the theatre ... life.
MARTIN. You've got me confused with two other fellows.
JAN. I think it's wonderful. I'm very proud of you.
MARTIN. Well, that's presumptuous enough, anyway.
JAN. Isn't it pretty, the lawn? Michael and I are breaking up.
MARTIN. Breaking up?
JAN. *(Nods.)* It isn't working.
MARTIN. It isn't working. It isn't working. Marvelous expression, isn't it? Covers it all. Says it succinctly and to the point. It isn't working. What a pleasure to hear that! You're not a bad sort.
JAN. Aren't I? Then why do I appear to be so damned un-

lovable?

MARTIN. That could be anything — personality, wardrobe, hair.

JAN. Oh, thanks.

MARTIN. Where's Karen?

JAN. Who's Karen?

MARTIN. Karen. Oh, such a nice girl.

JAN. You mean that friend I had in college?

MARTIN. Such a nice girl.

JAN. What about her?

MARTIN. You might have been happier as a lesbian. Possibly not, no, they seem so troubled these days. Always marching about carrying banners.

JAN. I just don't happen to be a lesbian, Daddy.

MARTIN. Such a pity. It might make you more energetic.

JAN. *(Laughs.)* You remember that poem you wrote?

MARTIN. Poem?

JAN. About Sappho? About the two ladies sitting on a cloud and caressing one another while they discussed the state of the arts? Terribly moving. And informative. The arts were in a dreadful state.

MARTIN. Shhh! I hear worms. Do you hear them?

JAN. No, I don't hear worms.

MARTIN. You really should consult a good ear man. The hearing of worms is vital, at least in a civilized person. But who's civilized nowadays?

JAN. Yes. True. *(Sighs; after a moment.)* I feel awfully lost. I love Michael, but he's apparently fallen out of love with me.

MARTIN. You've always had a tendency to make too much of things. It puts me off.

JAN. I'm sorry.

MARTIN. And the lawn isn't pretty at all. That boy has hit puberty on us and we're to be left with very long blades of grass. Very long. They'll be over our heads one of these days. And I hope *then* you'll be satisfied. *(Felicia appears carrying a tray with three small glasses, each with a cube of ice in it.)*

FELICIA. Here we are. I put a cube of ice in each glass since the bottle isn't cold.

JAN. Wonderful.

FELICIA. *(Puts tray on table.)* Now, if you'll open it, Jan.

JAN. *(Opening it.)* Of course.

FELICIA. It's a little early in the day for the hard stuff, but there are some days when I think one should have the hard stuff early.

MARTIN. She can't hear the worms.

FELICIA. Really?

JAN. Can you?

FELICIA. Well, of course, I can. No, no ... *(Jan is pouring.)* ... not too much for me, dear. *Or* your father.

JAN. Is it bad for him?

FELICIA. A little does wonders. Too much works the other way.

MARTIN. What is it?

JAN. It's vodka, Daddy.

MARTIN. Vodka?

FELICIA. You remember, darling, how much we used to love our vodka martinis?

JAN. Why do you keep asking him if he remembers?

FELICIA. Because sometimes he does, Jan, he really does. And that can be very exciting.

MARTIN. Vodka.

FELICIA. *(Hands Martin glass.)* Now, Martin, you can hold it and drink it.

MARTIN. Gratified desires.

FELICIA. *(Laughs.)* That's right. *(They are all seated, Martin between the two ladies so that they talk across him, and they all have drinks.)* Now, shall we have a toast? Yes. What shall we toast?

MARTIN. To Michael.

FELICIA. Well, at the moment, I'm not sure that's —

JAN. Oh, why not? *(Lifts glass.)* To Michael.

MARTIN. He's steady, that's the thing. You'll appreciate that in later life. Money coming in every Thursday. *(Sips.)* Gratified desires.

FELICIA. It's delicious. I've often thought of becoming an alcoholic. I don't know why I haven't. Too much to do, I suppose.

MARTIN. He's steady.
JAN. Yes, Daddy.
MARTIN. You'll appreciate that in later life.
FELICIA. *(To Jan.)* How's the job? Martin, darling, try not to spill.
MARTIN. He's steady.
JAN. It's fine. I get a little bored sometimes, but ...
FELICIA. Well, there are worse things.
JAN. Do you ever get out, Mother?
FELICIA. Of course I do. When Mary's here I do the shopping. Get what we need. Isn't that right, Martin? You like Mary.
MARTIN. The reputed mother of Jesus.
FELICIA. Not that one. The one who comes to clean.
MARTIN. I had thought they were one and the same. That having gone through immaculate conception, which can take it out of one, she had fallen on hard times and was reduced to doing the dusting. *(Jan and Felicia both laugh.)*
FELICIA. Maybe so. I'll ask her next time she comes.
MARTIN. The plague making us as cruel as dogs one to another.
FELICIA. Your father is fascinated by calamities. He sees them as cataclysmic, but in a curious way. Don't you, dear?
MARTIN. I see *you!*
FELICIA. And I see *you! (To Jan.)* Is a salad all right? And I've got a nice cold soup. And ice cream for after, but ... *(She mouths "no chocolate sauce" silently.)*
JAN. Who needs it? Wonderful.
MARTIN. Whispers ... whispers.
FELICIA. *(Puts hand on Martin's knee.)* Sorry, darling.
MARTIN. *(Slaps at Felicia's hand.)* I do hate it when you touch me!
FELICIA. I know you do, dear, and I'll try not to.
JAN. Oh, God ...
FELICIA. No, it's not so bad. It's not so bad. I have him, anyway. He isn't dead and I'm not alone.
MARTIN. Very good news.
JAN. You have to have some life of your own.

FELICIA. Well, what do you think this is? If Martin isn't my life, what is he?

MARTIN. That's what I wonder.

JAN. He could go into a home.

FELICIA. He's *in* a home!

MARTIN. I abhor fussing. I don't mind debating, however. If you wish to debate, I shall sit quietly and listen … and learn … and grow.

FELICIA. There's nothing to debate.

JAN. We've talked about it, Gary and Mark and I.

FELICIA. What you talk about is your own business. What I do with my life is mine. Is that understood? I appreciate your concern and that's that.

MARTIN. Isn't she cranky! I should like another drink.

FELICIA. I'm afraid not, Martin.

MARTIN. I want another drink!

FELICIA. I said no. It'll make you too excited. *(Martin rises suddenly.)*

MARTIN. You really are an old witch! *(He moves unsteadily in the opposite direction from the house and disappears offstage.)*

FELICIA. *(Calls.)* Where are you going?

MARTIN. *(From offstage.)* I'm off to see the wizard! *(Jan has gotten up and looks after Martin.)*

FELICIA. What's he doing?

JAN. He isn't doing anything. He's stopped by the willow tree.

FELICIA. Is he crying, Jan, can you see?

JAN. No. He's just standing there. I can see him from here. *(She sits, facing in the direction Martin has gone.)*

FELICIA. He's probably listening to the worms. Keep an eye on him. I want the rest of my drink.

JAN. *(Lifts bottle.)* Would you like a bit more?

FELICIA. *(Holds out glass.)* Yes. Please. It seems mean when I wouldn't let Martin, but it really isn't good for him. And I think it is for me, of course. You know, dear, it's curious, but I don't think of myself as old. Oh, I have all the aches and pains, of course, but I don't *feel* old. That woman in the mirror has nothing to do with me. Not what's inside, you know.

But we *are* old and it might be better if we faced our ages and said well, we're so near the end, anyway, let's get it over with. But I can't seem to accept that there isn't something more, no matter what the quality of it may be. That doesn't mean I haven't thought of it. I got in touch with the euthanasia people.

JAN. Mother!

FELICIA. Well, it seemed prudent. Have them send the literature. Find out how it's done. Go together was the idea, the two of us, hand in hand walking into the sunset. Rather romantic. I imagined violins playing. All very neatly managed. It would really be the best thing. I couldn't go on without Martin. And, of course, he wouldn't last without me. Why not just do it?

JAN. You mustn't think like that.

FELICIA. Well, I don't. Not any more. My, this is good vodka! You really shouldn't spend your money on us. No, there's something to be said for struggling on. I'm not quite sure what, but something. Oh, I know he won't get better ... that's not realistic ... but do you know I think there's still a chance of ... of ...

JAN. Of what, mother?

FELICIA. I don't know. It's selfish of me, I suppose. To think our number isn't up. Work to do yet. Fun to be had. To think we deserve that. Appalling, really, when you think of the young being struck down by this awful AIDS thing. Bright little babies with just two years of life ahead of them. Who do I think we are? Especially when you consider what we've had.

JAN. Yes.

FELICIA. Almost 40 years of it.

JAN. We used to be jealous of you.

FELICIA. Who?

JAN. We were. Gary and Mark and me.

FELICIA. Jealous? Of what?

JAN. Well, I don't know exactly. You didn't seem to need us, really.

FELICIA. *(Bristling.)* Oh, my dear, I hope you don't think ... well, really, you were never neglected!

JAN. No, no. It was just that you loved each other so much.
FELICIA. *(After a long moment.)* What's he doing? Can you see him?
JAN. *(Nods.)* He's just standing there.
FELICIA. He's not … doing anything, is he?
JAN. Like what?
FELICIA. Well, sometimes he just forgets and opens his trousers and relieves himself.
JAN. Oh, God!
FELICIA. I worry about the neighbors. He seems absolutely oblivious. Great dignity. Quite beautifully done, but still we can't have that.
JAN. No. It's another reason why you should consider —
FELICIA. Do you know I thought next year we'd have marigolds. All along there. A vast sea of golden marigolds. Yes, I'm determined. My thumb isn't as green as I'd like, but I am determined.
JAN. He's coming back.
FELICIA. Oh, that's good.
JAN. He looks furious.
FELICIA. *(Wearily.)* Oh, my dear. *(Martin appears, goes right to the table.)*
MARTIN. What are we having? Cocktails? Well, I'll have one! *(He grabs the bottle and pours into his glass, spilling, of course.)*
FELICIA. Now do be careful, Martin.
MARTIN. *(Sits, sips.)* Well, doesn't that hit the spot! What is it?
JAN. It's vodka, Daddy.
FELICIA. You remember how we used to enjoy our vodka martinis? Now, we must go in to lunch in a moment.
MARTIN. Not during the cocktail hour! No, no, no! This is that lovely twilight time when we relax after the day's labors. I shall unwind before your very eyes. You'll see a change. *(Looks over lawn.)* Oh, my God! More dead! More dead!
FELICIA. Martin …
MARTIN. *(To Jan.)* Caravans of them, carrying their corpses on great stretcher-like conveyances. Oh, the smell! And they have no concern for the fitness of things. They *will* come dur-

ing the cocktail hour. Well, we must ignore them.

FELICIA. Martin ...

MARTIN. We shall pay them no mind. I do think that's the worst possible taste, don't you? Parading their dead past us while we're trying to have a quiet drink? I shall write a piece.

FELICIA. Now, Martin, as soon as you've finished that, we're going in and we'll have lunch and —

MARTIN. *(Puts back head, closes eyes, recites.)*

"I went to the garden of love,
And saw what I never had seen;
A chapel was built in the midst,
Where I used to play on the green

And the gates of this chapel were shut,
And "Thou shalt not" writ over the door;
So I turn'd to the garden of love
That so many sweet flowers bore

And I saw it was filled with graves,
And tombstones where flowers should be;
And priests in black gowns were walking their rounds,
And binding with briars my joys and desires."

(Opens his eyes.) Oh, isn't that a wonder! "And binding with briars my joys and desires." How beautiful! Oh, to have written that!

FELICIA. Yes! Beautiful!

JAN. Who wrote that, Daddy?

MARTIN. A genius.

JAN. Who?

MARTIN. I ... I ...

FELICIA. *(As Martin looks blank.)* You remember, darling. It's William Blake.

MARTIN. *(An explosion.)* Why do you do that to me? Why? Oh, well, of course it's because I'm such a bloody *flop,* isn't it!

FELICIA. All I said was —

MARTIN. Tell the whole world! Show me for the triple-plated failure I am, is that it?

FELICIA. No, Martin, no, no..

MARTIN. You think I don't see what you're up to? Call me a writer? Call me a poet? Call me a critic? Who? Who? Me? Tell them then! Let them see that we're dying! Tell them words are nothing now! Nothing now! Oh, do you think when they carry the corpses across the lawn they put it in writing? They send out memos? No. No words! They're still as death and why not? Degrade first the arts if you'd mankind degrade! Do you hear me?

FELICIA. Martin, please.

MARTIN. I have more to say. It is a known fact that if you ride a bicycle you must keep the tires pumped up.

JAN. *(Laughs.)* Yes, Daddy.

MARTIN. Oh, shall we laugh? There is in existence on this planet a religious sect that believes the road to heaven is gained by puncturing automobile tires. Isn't it priceless? Well, it makes as much sense as anything else, doesn't it?

FELICIA. I did read something ...

MARTIN. As much sense as anything else. Do you hear the worms laughing? God knows there's no practice in the realm of religion so bizarre that somebody won't practice it. Oh, the human race! The human race! The human race!

FELICIA. After lunch, Martin, I think if you lie down —

MARTIN. Oh yes, why should I be ambulatory? Lay me down. Shut me up. What is this place? Why here of all places? Can't you tell the living from the dead? But look at that! If you look at the sun and then down at the trees, what do you see?

JAN. What do you see, Daddy?

MARTIN. Oh, I see it all *blindingly*. No difference. Not today, not tomorrow, not yesterday. A thousand years — no difference. Caught. Impaled. Yes, here. The child is father of the man. Who wrote that? Oh, I used to remember everything. I miss my memory. However, you mustn't be deceived. Everything is here, just in the back of the head. Kept. Recorded. Never erased. Despite the fact that I can't remember it, what does that matter? It is there. Kept. Kept. Such a multitude of people. Can you hear me? Not a moment gone! Not a conversation lost! Everything within me and I might say ... *(To Jan.)* ... within you and within what's-her-name. Oh dear, the dead! A thousand years! Two thousand! Three! It doesn't matter, you see. A fiery ball whirling through the universe and it's cocktail hour. Isn't it amusing?

JAN. Is it, Daddy?

MARTIN. Oh, I'm sure. Levity. Most important. *(He suddenly starts, sits up.)* Ah, did you see that?

FELICIA. What, Martin?

MARTIN. A man! Just now! Running across the grass!

FELICIA. No, I don't think so, dear.

MARTIN. Oh yes. Weeping for his child. Dead of the plague, I expect. Why do we weep? Why do we rejoice? How do we know who is here and who is not?

FELICIA. Shall we go in?

MARTIN. What for? To nibble lettuce? Not me! I'm going to have another gin, my dear ladies.

FELICIA. No, Martin, now you've had enough.

MARTIN. Do I have to use brute force on you, white woman?

JAN. Please, Daddy, let's go in.

MARTIN. I can tell you my heart sinks. It really does. Just like in bad literature, my heart sinks. When I think of it. To have spent so much time. So much effort. All of my life, really, under the lamp, scribbling away. Eye strain. Headaches. And for what? Not a poet, major, minor. A creator? Not me, no. Amateur at best. Essays. Light. A few impressions. No more than travelogues. Like slide lectures. See Venice, but not in January. Big deal. Criticism? Oh my, yes. Carping away. Grousing. Cut them down to my size. Confuse the public. Get high prices for the worst and leave the best to languish in disgrace, eh, Mr. Blake? Well, then, what have I created? A reputation. Mine! Nobody else's. Only mine. Meaningless, all of it! Worth nothing! I spit on it all! Get me out of here! Call me a cab!

FELICIA. Now, calm down, Martin.

MARTIN. *(To Jan.)* Did what's-her-name tell you I saw a vision of Christ himself? Oh, yes, I did. The other evening as I was gobbling down my dinner Jesus Christ appeared in the doorway of the dining room and do you know what he said to me?

JAN. What?

MARTIN. He said, "eat slower." Now I ask you!

FELICIA. Very good advice. Now, come along, Martin. *(She rises.)* We're going in, Jan.

JAN. Can you understand what I say, Daddy, when I tell you that you illuminated ... interpreted and illuminated ... the arts for thousands of people? You made them see! You showed them how to appreciate! I suppose you made your mistakes, but I can't remember you ever ... *ever* ...

MARTIN. That pullover's a very good color for you. You should wear it more often.

JAN. Listen to me! I can't remember you *ever* praising the bad or damning the good! You're a glorious success! And we love you!

MARTIN. You're very pretty. Did you ever know my wife? *(Felicia gives a little gasp.)*

JAN. *(Softly.)* Hush, mother. *(To Martin.)* No, I didn't. Tell me about her.

MARTIN. Oh, she was a saint. Beautiful beyond belief and a delicacy of thought that was like the morning sun breaking through the clouds. A most remarkable woman. And great fun, you know. I ... I ...

JAN. You what, Daddy?

MARTIN. I ... I ... I don't remember. *(Rises briskly.)* I believe I'm going in to lunch. Yes. Goodbye to you. *(He walks past Felicia and disappears in the direction of the house. Felicia looks at Jan for a moment and then smiles.)*

FELICIA. You see, dear Jan? A little longer. *(She turns and exits toward the house. The lights begin to fade as Jan rises and comes D. to address the audience.)*

JAN. I watched as my mother turned and followed my father into the house. On a cold February evening not long after, she suffered a stroke and died suddenly and lies buried in the village cemetery almost within view of our garden. My father lived on for three more years, but he never noticed she was gone. Michael did not return into my life, nor was anyone else to take his place. I haven't minded especially, except … except when I see the trees. In my heart's memory there will always be trees. There will always be shadows. But beneath those trees and in those shadows … as in an aging photograph … I see two remarkable people. And I hear laughter. And love seems to me to be the sunlight shining through the leaves. *(The lights go to black and the curtain falls.)*

THE END

PROPERTY LIST

Watch (FELICIA)
Brown paper bag with bottle (JAN)
Tray (FELICIA) with:
   3 small glasses, each with an ice cube

The Librarian

✓5) Libraries
/5) Mental illness

/ Drama set in mental institution
Librarian driven to act of violence
when her beloved library was closed

/ 1m 2w 1 interior

THE LIBRARIAN was first produced as a reading by the American Conservatory Theater (Edward W. Hastings, Artistic Director) in San Francisco, in April, 1991. It was directed by Craig Slaight. The cast was as follows:

ROSE PENMORE ....Julie Harris
VOICE (DOCTOR) ....Peter Donat
NURSE ....Joyce Ebert

THE LIBRARIAN was presented at the Morgan-Wixson Theatre in Los Angeles, California, in April, 1995. It was directed by George Schaefer. The cast was as follows:

ROSE PENMORE ....Julie Harris
VOICE (DOCTOR) ....Russ Petranto
NURSE ....Joan Crosby

The Librarian

An empty stage except that there is a suggestion of something clinical about it — perhaps a whiteness — that means bureaucracy and sterility. Cold. Against the bare back wall projections might be shown, if one wished. There is a door stage right and a window stage left or — again — they are suggested. There is a table stage left and three or four chairs, probably metallic, possibly folding.

As the lights come up, Miss Rose Penmore is seated on a chair stage center, facing the audience. She is a lady in her sixties, I should think, simply dressed in a skirt and blouse. She is rather delicate and pretty; one would readily take her for a librarian. And yet — although she sits primly with her ankles crossed — the rest of her body slumps oddly. Her hands are in her lap, but her head is slightly tilted and her eyes are closed. She seems to be asleep or, worse, bordering on unconsciousness.

A voice addresses her from the front of the house, a voice that is masculine and firm. It seems to come from a loudspeaker.

VOICE. Miss Penmore? Miss Penmore? Can you hear me, Miss Penmore? Miss Penmore? *(Calls.)* Nurse! Nurse! *(A matronly Nurse enters. She's bustling and a little tough, but not unkind.)*
NURSE. *(Looks toward voice.)* Yes, doctor?
VOICE. I can't seem to get through to her.
NURSE. She had a shot.
VOICE. *(Wearily.)* She's not supposed to have medication before interrogation.
NURSE. I know. It was a mistake. I'm sorry. These things happen. *(She rubs Rose's hands.)* Miss Penmore! Miss Penmore!

Come on, dear, doctor's waiting. Rose!

VOICE. I can't see her again until a week from Thursday. *(Rose has made a sound and a move.)*

NURSE. I think she's coming around.

VOICE. There are too many mistakes being made.

NURSE. She'll be all right. She's really quite perky when she's ... Miss Penmore, doctor wants to talk to you! *(Rose opens her eyes. She is startled, jumps slightly.)*

ROSE. Oh! Am I home?

NURSE. No, dear, you're in the hospital and the doctor just wants to ask you a few questions.

VOICE. Good morning, Miss Penmore.

NURSE. She'll be all right now. *(She watches a moment, then exits.)*

VOICE. Can you hear me, Miss Penmore?

ROSE. I'm sorry. I must have dozed ...

VOICE. They gave you a shot. They felt you needed it.

ROSE. I must have needed it.

VOICE. I'm sure you did. They don't make mistakes. Do you feel up to answering a few questions for me?

ROSE. I've always enjoyed answering questions.

VOICE. Good. Are you comfortable?

ROSE. Perfectly. Thank you.

VOICE. Now, let's see, you are Miss Rose Penmore.

ROSE. Yes.

VOICE. You are a single lady?

ROSE. Yes.

VOICE. You've worked, have you, Miss Penmore? An occupation?

ROSE. Yes.

VOICE. What was that?

ROSE. *(Rises unsteadily.)* I am a librarian.

VOICE. Please remain seated. *(Rose sits.)* And how long were you a librarian, Miss Penmore?

ROSE. I am a librarian.

VOICE. How long was that for?

ROSE. I am still a librarian.

VOICE. Your employment was for what period of time?

ROSE. I have worked as a librarian for 38 years. Not very long, is it?
VOICE. It seems long enough.
ROSE. Oh no. Years wasted. I should have started earlier. I would have had I realized.
VOICE. Realized what?
ROSE. That I was a librarian.
VOICE. And where were you employed?
ROSE. Here.
VOICE. Here?
ROSE. Not here. I don't mean here. I'm not entirely sure where I am. In this state. I think.
VOICE. What town would that be?
ROSE. Lanckton.
VOICE. Oh, yes. About 40 minutes from here.
ROSE. I would think longer.
VOICE. Possibly an hour.
ROSE. I don't speed.
VOICE. A small town.
ROSE. Not really small. But not growing. Industrial primarily. Not a bit attractive, most people think. But home, of course.
VOICE. Your family is there?
ROSE. Robert. My brother Robert.
VOICE. Oh, yes, he's the one who ...
ROSE. ... signed the papers. Robert. He had me committed.
VOICE. You're not locked up, you know, Miss Penmore. You don't see bars on the windows, do you?
ROSE. No.
VOICE. There's not wire meshing everywhere. You don't see guards and guns, do you?
ROSE. No.
VOICE. Well, then ...
ROSE. Does that mean I'm free to leave?
VOICE. *(After a pause.)* Don't you like it here? *(No answer.)* Do you know why you're here?
ROSE. Of course. I'm here because I'm a danger to myself

and to others.

VOICE. Do you consider yourself a danger to yourself and to others?

ROSE. Yes.

VOICE. Why is that?

ROSE. Perfectly clear. I tend toward violence.

VOICE. And why is that? I say, why is that? Can you answer that?

ROSE. I'm a librarian.

VOICE. Can you answer my question?

ROSE. I'm a librarian.

VOICE. I can't say that I think of librarians as violent generally.

ROSE. I'm surprised that you think of them at all. Oh, I'm sorry.

VOICE. That's all right.

ROSE. I want to cooperate. I can think rather quickly, but I sometimes speak before I think. I don't want to hurt anyone's feelings.

VOICE. Don't worry about that. *(A mild joke.)* We're not supposed to *have* any feelings.

ROSE. Well, that must be easier.

VOICE. You never married, Miss Penmore?

ROSE. No.

VOICE. And why is that?

ROSE. I suppose the reason I've never married is that nobody ever asked me. That's normally the reason women don't marry, isn't it? And I really don't quite understand that. I don't care for bragging, but I do feel I'm reasonably attractive and fairly bright and of ... of, well, of quite a loving nature ... and when you look around and see what *other* people marry ... well, I do sometimes wonder why I wasn't snapped up.

VOICE. Perhaps you didn't really want to be ... snapped up.

ROSE. In that case I should at least have liked the satisfaction of refusing someone. Is it very warm in here?

VOICE. Are you too warm? We'll see if the heat can be turned down. *(Aside.)* See if the heat can be turned down, would you, please?

ROSE. Jane Austen didn't marry.

VOICE. I'm sorry. What was that, Miss Penmore?

ROSE. Jane Austen never married.

VOICE. I see. Thank you.

ROSE. She didn't find it a lack. At least she's never mentioned it to me. She had her work, you see. I am a librarian. And while I think one naturally has moments of loneliness, one is simply too occupied to dwell on it. Work is the important thing, you see. Other things are peripheral. Pleasant, but peripheral. Do you know I believe it's cooler already! Is that possible? It's probably just me. I'm cold and then I'm hot and then I'm cold again. Please don't have them running back and forth to the thermostat.

VOICE. I wonder if I heard you right, Miss Penmore. You said Jane Austen never *mentioned* it to you?

ROSE. Oh, dear. I really must stop doing that. You'll lock me up forever.

VOICE. Jane Austen is dead, isn't she?

ROSE. Yes, dear doctor, she died in July of 1817. I'm sorry if you weren't informed.

VOICE. And yet you implied that she speaks to you.

ROSE. I didn't imply a thing. I merely said she never mentioned to me that she felt a lack in never marrying. Considering that she died in 1817, it would have been very odd if she *had* mentioned it to me, wouldn't it?

VOICE. *(Rather thrown.)* Well, I ... I ...

ROSE. She wrote a beautiful prayer, by the way, toward the end. I think I can remember it. "Incline us, oh God, to think humbly of ourselves, to be serene only in the examination of our own conduct, to consider our fellow creatures with kindness, and to judge of all they say and do with that charity which we would desire from them ourselves." Do you think humbly of yourself?

VOICE. Miss Penmore, if we may —

ROSE. She had to remind herself to be humble, you see, because she was a satirist and satirists don't incline to be charitable.

VOICE. You've been living with your brother, have you?
ROSE. Yes.
VOICE. And his family?
ROSE. I am his family.
VOICE. Your brother's also single?
ROSE. Yes. Do you see us as hopelessly undesirable?
VOICE. He was never ... snapped up?
ROSE. He's been snapped up several times, I believe, but he's never married.
VOICE. Why do you think that is?
ROSE. Well, I've pondered it over and over in my mind and I think the reason in all probability is that he isn't heterosexual.
VOICE. Oh.
ROSE. Yes. Oh. I think what most strikes home in Jane's little prayer is the phrase, "to consider our fellow creatures with kindness," don't you?
VOICE. And you and your brother share a house?
ROSE. Small house. Until my mother died, there were three of us. We weren't happy, if that's your next question. My mother was not an easy woman to live with. May I stand for a moment?
VOICE. Of course.
ROSE. *(Rises.)* I do get stiff sitting.
VOICE. Did you love your mother?
ROSE. Oh dear, aren't we getting down to Psychology One! Would you define love for me, please?
VOICE. Did you care deeply for your mother?
ROSE. I cared for her, if that's the same thing, all those years. Fed her, cleaned her, bathed her. Tried to love her, wanted to love her. Finally gave up. It's a very terrible thing, isn't it, to have a mother who is ...
VOICE. Yes?
ROSE. ... without compassion. And yet she must be tended in old age, nurtured, cared for, if not deeply. Luckily I had Vincent.
VOICE. Vincent? Who's Vincent?
ROSE. I'm sorry. I do mean to cooperate, but there are

some things you simply wouldn't understand.

VOICE. Try to be honest with me, Miss Penmore. We're attempting to get to the root of your problem. Let me be the judge of what I will understand.

ROSE. Certainly. Of course. I'll try not to keep secrets from you. *(At window.)* Can you see? It's snowing outside. Oh I just had the strangest feeling! It's January and gray and cold and snowing and I'm in a photograph ... an aging photograph ... fifty years from now ... a hundred years from now ... and a young man is holding the photograph ... and studying it ... and he is saying, "Do you see this photograph? A woman ... looking out a window ... at the snow. See how she gazes at the falling snow! I wonder who she was?" And he will raise the photograph to his lips and kiss it tenderly.

VOICE. Please sit down, Miss Penmore.

ROSE. *(Sitting.)* And I will have been in my coffin all those decades. I will have been dead for a hundred years when he falls in love with me. My throat is so dry.

VOICE. Would you like a glass of water?

ROSE. That would be pleasant.

VOICE. *(Calls.)* Nurse! Nurse!

ROSE. How I wish I had known her, he'll say. *(Nurse enters.)*

NURSE. Yes, doctor?

VOICE. Would you bring Miss Penmore a glass of water, please?

NURSE. Oh, sure. *(She exits.)*

VOICE. About your tendency toward violence ...

ROSE. Yes?

VOICE. Does it manifest itself often?

ROSE. I would consider once often, wouldn't you? It's getting warm again.

VOICE. I should like to hear about it if you'd like to tell me.

ROSE. Is there any point really? I'm capable of murder. What more is there to say? Except that I do feel I'm not unique. I'm surprised to arrive at that conclusion, but I do feel any one of us is capable of murder given the right conditions. Man is a killer. I'm sorry if that upsets your little

applecart and I don't take pleasure in saying it, but it's true.
VOICE. You don't believe in the goodness of man?
ROSE. *(Sudden anger, rises.) Oh, leave me alone!* Where is that water?
VOICE. If you don't stay calm they'll have to give you another injection.
ROSE. They can give me all the injections they like, but that won't change things, will it!
VOICE. It will change your outlook.
ROSE. I don't suppose you've heard of Anne Frank?
VOICE. I've heard of Anne Frank.
ROSE. Well ... well, in the midst of torture and degradation and the death of millions of innocents ... bodies of men, women and children ... aunts, uncles, cousins, lovers ... artists, composers, authors ... a Beethoven ... a Shakespeare ... pushed into the ovens ... mountains and mountains of sweet and good people ... in the midst of that Anne Frank sat and wrote, "In spite of everything, I still believe in the goodness of people." Does that lift your heart? *(Very angrily.) Does that give you hope? (The Nurse enters, brings a glass of water to Rose.)*
NURSE. Here you are, Miss Penmore.
ROSE. *(Takes it.)* Thank you.
VOICE. Please sit down, Miss Penmore.
ROSE. *(Sips, sits.)* Yes, of course.
NURSE. *(To Voice.)* Shall I wait for the glass?
VOICE. I don't think so. Miss Penmore won't fling it at me, will you, Miss Penmore?
ROSE. I hadn't planned to. *(Nurse shrugs and exits.)*
VOICE. Better?
ROSE. *(Smiles, nods.)* My throat gets so dry.
VOICE. We could take a break, but it's a bit early. We haven't gotten very far, have we?
ROSE. Haven't we?
VOICE. Not as far as I'd like. *(Rose, having finished the water, holds up the glass, indicates table.)*
ROSE. Shall I...?
VOICE. Just put it anywhere. On the floor or ... *(But she is up and putting it on the table.)* ... that's fine. *(Rose puts the glass*

on the table, but remains standing, her back to the audience. She is suddenly ominously still.) Now, Miss Penmore, let's ... *(Hesitates.)* ... Miss Penmore? *(No sound or move.)* Miss Penmore? *(Rose turns slowly. She is slightly different, slightly stranger.)*

ROSE. Sometimes, you know, in the afternoons when the school children have come and gone ... there's a quiet period in the library ... a lull before the evening when the adults come in. And I sit at my desk ... Vincent is generally somewhere near me in the stacks or at the periodicals ... and Anne will come in and I chat with her just as I would with the other children. She's so bright and fun-loving. We do laugh over her statement about the goodness of people. She does see now, of course, the irony of it. I stroke her hair sometimes, although one really must be a bit on one's guard against that sort of thing. People are so ready to misunderstand, aren't they? She kissed me once, ever so lightly on the cheek, and I must tell you for days ... for days I saw the world for what it might have been ... in a kind of eternal sunlight ... great rays of it that flooded down upon me until I was enfolded in the warmth of large dove-like wings ... and quite ... and quite faint from little whispers of love. *(New mood, brusquely.)* I have put the glass on the table. *(Sits.)* You are safe. I won't fling it at you.

VOICE. Was it a nice childhood?

ROSE. *(Knowingly.)* Oh.

VOICE. Was it a nice childhood?

ROSE. No, doctor, I wasn't abused or mistreated or neglected so we can't blame me on that. Mother may have been without compassion, but she rather liked children. It was adults she didn't take to. My father among them. But he died fairly young, thereby escaping her sharp tongue early. I think we can say that I had a perfectly normal childhood. As, I might add, did my brother.

VOICE. Does his homosexuality upset you?

ROSE. On the contrary, it delights me.

VOICE. Really?

ROSE. He's the most enchanting man I know. He was filled

with laughter and fun even when mother was at her worst. I love him and he loves me.

VOICE. But he had you committed.

ROSE. I said he loves me.

VOICE. You don't resent that?

ROSE. I'm a danger to myself and others. Robert is very strong. He has put me out of harm's way at, I'm sure, an enormous expense to his heart ... not to mention his pocketbook. He wants me back ... *me* ... not the hatchet woman.

VOICE. Hatchet?

ROSE. I am a librarian.

VOICE. Tell me about Vincent.

ROSE. I'm sorry.

VOICE. Why not?

ROSE. Because he's suffered enough. Read his letters. It's all there.

VOICE. Who is he?

ROSE. If you listen, really listen, you can hear him talking. *(Slightly different voice.)* I can do very well without God in my life, but I cannot, ill as I am, do without something that is greater than I, which is my life — the power to create. *(Her own voice.)* I listen to him always. He comes to me in the dark and I cradle him in my arms and sometimes ... oh, how we do laugh! Because I quote prices to him. Ten million for this one! Twenty million for that one! He laughs until he cries. He can laugh, you see, we can laugh together because ... because ...

VOICE. Because?

ROSE. Because it's a laughing matter now. It wasn't then.

VOICE. *(Pronounces it Go.)* Van Gogh?

ROSE. We prefer the Dutch pronunciation. Van Guck.

VOICE. Excuse me.

ROSE. We're not unbending.

VOICE. Miss Penmore, so far you've mentioned three names, I believe — Jane Austen, Anne Frank and Vincent Van Guck — all of whom are dead and all of whom you profess to have known and spoken to.

ROSE. Yes?

VOICE. Would it surprise you then if I were to draw certain conclusions regarding your mental state?
ROSE. Not at all. You think me crazy as a coot.
VOICE. Not a phrase we generally use in our profession, but not far from ...
ROSE. Well, you are wrong.
VOICE. You told me that you're a danger to yourself and to others.
ROSE. But I didn't say I was crazy. Disturbed. I admit to that. I am disturbed. May I ask you a question?
VOICE. What is it?
ROSE. Is it possible that in your entire life you have never had friends who are dead?
VOICE. I have friends, of course, who have died.
ROSE. No friends you have never known alive?
VOICE. I'm afraid not.
ROSE. Your experience has been limited. Perhaps we should change places. Oh dear, I mustn't talk like that! I do apologize.
VOICE. That's all right. I can't be offended.
ROSE. Apparently not.
VOICE. Now, Miss Penmore, can we investigate the causes behind your ... *(Aside to someone.)* ... what? Oh, thank you. *(Into speaker.)* Miss Penmore, would you just remain comfortable for a moment? They've just given me further records on you.
ROSE. Really? I feel quite important. Would it be all right if I were to walk around a bit? In the room, I mean?
VOICE. Certainly. *(She rises and begins slowly to circle the room. She speaks half to herself, finally, and half to him, but she continues to walk around the room.)*
ROSE. I don't like the cold. Never have. It frightens me. I can imagine dying in it. Virginia drowned, you know. Put rocks in her pockets and walked into the river. Virginia is my closest friend ... my closest woman friend, that is ... closer than Jane even. Virginia Woolf. I suppose that's because we're more contemporary. The centuries *can* separate one, although I've never felt that with my dear George Sand. Her passion and mine are as one, despite what you see before you ... my

clothes and demeanor. The years make no difference. Time is nonexistent. I think that's where we lose our way, don't you? We live only within our own time whereas actually, if we troubled, we could move in and out of the centuries ... lunch with Louis the XIV at Versailles and dinner with Cole Porter at the Waldorf-Astoria if we troubled? If we freed our minds? With Virginia as we walk over the downs, a stick in her hand, a dog at our heels, and we speak in the soft English mist, our minds are as one. And when I am with Virginia the world around me is enhanced. The sky above is bluer ... the grass below is greener ...

VOICE. Miss Penmore, would you sit down now, please?

ROSE. *(Sits.)* Of course.

VOICE. I now see a little better what we're dealing with.

ROSE. Progress.

VOICE. I'll make my questions more direct.

ROSE. They didn't seem *in*direct.

VOICE. The name of your library ... was ...

ROSE. It's the Mabel Truesdale Smith Library on Deming Street. Not a very good neighborhood, I'm afraid ... down by the river ... industrial ... and the people are, on the whole, poor. I suppose one might even say impoverished. Various ethnic groups are clustered there in uneasy relationships that sometimes burst into actual warfare. But I like the people very much. I find them to have a kind of energy that's attractive. Some are lazy, of course, and many don't want to learn, but that's why it's so important that we be there — the library, I mean. As an example. To open the door just a crack so they can see that there's a beautiful garden just beyond. And I might say that I have never, well, almost never felt fear in the library. Or driving home. There *was* a young man who attempted a very inept robbery one evening, but one of the burlier patrons simply took him out by the seat of the pants. And I have been ... occasionally ... the object of certain ... sexual ... allusions by the rougher element — a word, a whistle, a mysterious gesture — but that's rare and hardly important. Robert worries about me, but when you are surrounded by the great literature of the world danger seems very far away.

VOICE. There were some ... unpleasant incidences.

ROSE. Unpleasant incidences?

VOICE. You have a library board.

ROSE. Yes. Reasonable people, on the whole, with certain exceptions.

VOICE. There were difficulties?

ROSE. Is it warm again?

VOICE. Would you tell me about those difficulties?

ROSE. Whenever you have more than two people there are bound to be difficulties. When it becomes a committee you can multiply that by however many are on the committee. If it's a board you may add to that the complication of power and standing.

VOICE. Could we be a little more specific?

ROSE. I don't think so.

VOICE. You had an altercation with the board.

ROSE. A slight run-in. But it was all right in the end.

VOICE. I want to help you. I can't if you won't cooperate.

ROSE. I should like very much to have a little more water, if you don't mind.

VOICE. *(Sighs, then calls.)* Nurse! Nurse!

ROSE. I don't mean to be trouble.

VOICE. No trouble. *(Nurse enters.)* Miss Penmore would like more water. Why don't you just bring one of the pitchers?

NURSE. Thirsty, aren't we! *(She exits.)*

ROSE. My throat gets so dry. Also I'm not sleeping well. I wake up in the middle of the night and I think I'm home, you see, and then I realize I'm not and I ... and I panic just a little.

VOICE. Only a few more questions. Just to get at the source.

ROSE. Yes. The source.

VOICE. About the board ...

ROSE. Is she bringing the water?

VOICE. In a moment. What exactly was the slight run-in? With the board?

ROSE. Well, it wasn't with the board really. I mean that isn't how it began. It began with a certain woman ... a Mrs. Gorman. Rather a fanatic, I'm afraid. Frustrated, I suspect, in some way in her private life. A very hostile, belligerent woman who has taken up with a religious group. I don't remember what they call themselves, but they're very cheap, very theatrical and very vocal on one of the television stations. Fundamentalists, of course, and quite rabid. And uneducated, naturally, but determined to inflict their views on others. Who was it? Berenson, I believe, who said, "Every religion is a theocracy whose purpose is to impose its will on as much of the human race as it can approach." Yes, Berenson. In 1951. Rather good, isn't it?

VOICE. Mrs. Gorman?

ROSE. He would have been in his 87th year. Berenson. In 1951.

VOICE. Miss Penmore, *please* ...

ROSE. I'm sorry, but those little bits of information fly into one's head and I always think they should be shared. Mrs. Gorman. Oh dear, yes. She wrote a really vile letter on the letterhead of that fly-by-night religious organization and ... *(Nurse enters, puts pitcher on table.)* ... oh, thank you. I can pour. *(Rises, pours; Nurse exits.)* My throat gets so dry. *(Drinks.)* I can't seem to get enough. *(Pours more.)* My hands shake now. They never did before. *(Drinks, puts down glass.)* There. That's better. *(She sits, folds hands, smiles, faces him silently.)*

VOICE. She wrote a really vile letter.

ROSE. Yes.

VOICE. And?

ROSE. What's the point?

VOICE. Please continue. About the letter.

ROSE. The work of a madwoman, really. Books to be banned from the library lest they corrupt the morals of our youth. Not just the ones you might normally expect ... Mr. Darwin and his theory of evolution, for instance. So dangerous. The masses must be fed fables, not facts. Oh, no, an expanded list of low and disgusting volumes ranging from Salinger to Shakespeare with Mark Twain and James Joyce sandwiched in ... works of beauty, writing to illuminate the human heart and soul. I could hardly hold the letter in my hand I was so revolted. And I thought ... *(Looks around distractedly.)* ... I actually thought that once we were beyond the shock of this evil letter and had managed to keep our food down, we would shudder and shrug and go on about our business. Not at all. Not at all.

VOICE. Yes?

ROSE. Yes?

VOICE. You're doing very well. Please go on.

ROSE. Thank you for the kind words. Has the snow stopped? In weather like this my brother always keeps a fire going in the fireplace in our living room. So cheerful. There's something about a fire, don't you think?

VOICE. I have only so much time, Miss Penmore.

ROSE. Well, they trembled! They literally trembled! The board trembled! They considered. How to deal with it? What to do? It was religion, you see. The rolling of the eyes. Hushed voices. Religion! *(Loudly.)* Well, haven't you heard, I said, that patriotism is the last refuge of the scoundrel? And don't you know that the even more final refuge of the scoundrel ... the safest one of all ... is *religion?* Shocked silence. Had I meant, actually meant what I said? A nice woman like me? Oh, how Bernard Shaw would have laughed! How I wish he had walked in at that very moment and backed me up. He abhors board meetings, however. And I didn't need him, really, as it turned out. I had made my point. I had stemmed the tide. The letter was ultimately tabled and ignored.

VOICE. But there were further complications?

ROSE. *(Laughs.)* Oh, I must tell you! I don't generally watch television ... I find so much of it horrifying ... *that's* what our children shouldn't see ... but Robert likes to watch the late news and that very night we saw that the minister ... *Mrs. Gorman's minister* ... had dipped into the church funds to the tune of hundreds of thousands of dollars! Limousines, apparently, and fur coats for his heavily-painted wife and a mansion somewhere on the Florida coast and caught! Caught! He was caught! So you see?

VOICE. I see.

ROSE. Yes. Well. But. Do you remember ... I certainly do ... what it was like when we were young? Good and bad. Per-

fectly clear. Good and bad. Perfectly clear. Not a week later they appeared at the library, a great mob of them, led by the minister, *that* minister, Mrs. Gorman right behind him. They were following that minister, their minister ... still following him, you see ... because, do you see ... *it hadn't mattered!* Good or bad, it hadn't mattered. And there was the list held up before me. "We propose to remove these books from this library," said the minister. "And what do you propose to do with them?" I said. "We will build a fire and burn them," said he. "But don't you know," I said ... *(Rises.)* ... "that where books are burned, human beings will ultimately be burned?" I could smell the stench of burning flesh issuing from the chimneys of concentration camps. And he said, "We are of the faith!" And I said, "Well, we hear of corruption and we hear of faith, but when do we hear about *corrupt faith?*" *(She sits.)*
VOICE. Did you save the books?
ROSE. For the moment. They were content to kneel and pray ... for my soul, I suppose. They were very pitying of me. They did so wish to save me, you see, to show me the way. If there is good and evil, it occurred to me that day, it is not at all what we think it is. The devil is clever enough to employ many guises, including that of goodness. They left, yes. But one by one the books disappeared. First one was gone, then another. Then another. They were adept thieves.
VOICE. I'm sorry. You're tired. We won't be much longer. The violence ...
ROSE. Yes?
VOICE. The hatchet.
ROSE. Robert's. He uses it for the Christmas trees. I found it in the garage.
VOICE. And tell me what you did with it.
ROSE. I'm sorry. I don't remember.
VOICE. Shall I help you?
ROSE. I'm hoping ... if all goes well ... I'm hoping to be back at my desk by, well, I don't know. Shall I put a date on it? I only need a rest, I think, and then I can be back in the library by ... by mid April at the latest.
VOICE. There is no library, Miss Penmore.

ROSE. Am I too optimistic? Early May then.
VOICE. There is no library.
ROSE. *(A rush of words, a dizzying pace.)* My house here is painted the yellow color of fresh butter on the outside with glaringly green shutters it stands in the full sunlight in a square which has a green garden with plane trees oleanders and acacias and it is completely white-washed inside and the floor is made of red bricks and over it there is the intensely blue sky in this I can live and breathe meditate and paint!
VOICE. *There is no library.*
ROSE. *(Rises, screams.)* Vincent! *Vincent! (She breaks down and cries, sinks back into the chair.)*
VOICE. Miss Penmore! Are you all right? Miss Penmore? Shall I have the nurse give you an injection? Miss Penmore? Can you hear me? Can you talk to me? Can you tell me what happened?
ROSE. I'm all right. *(Slowly, softly.)* I arrived at the library one morning to discover a very startling discovery. There was no more money. In our great, rich, affluent country there was no more money. There was no money to maintain the library ... to pay the salaries ... to provide the books. I had been, you see, engaged in a battle to save a book here and a book there, while actually the war that would destroy all books everywhere was being fought and lost far beyond my little world, beyond anything I could recognize or comprehend. It was very simple — only a few words. "There is no more funding. We don't need religious fanatics to destroy you. We need not take sides, join factions. We need not explain. There is no more funding." The doors are locked. The books are gone. And if a child comes and says, "Please, Miss Penmore, what is truth? What is knowledge? What is beauty?" he is met with naked silence. The garden is no longer there.
VOICE. And what did you do?
ROSE. I went home. "Your services are no longer needed," they said. The young would not need me. The old would not need me. I went home. And there I remained for a day ... a week ... I can't say ... and I sat in blackness ... silent ... alone, except for my darling Robert. A week. Two weeks perhaps.

Utterly abandoned, I felt, by everything that had given meaning to my life. Until ... one evening ... just at twilight ... I heard a voice whispering into my ear. Vincent! Oh, how my heart soared! And then another voice ... Jane ... and then Anne ... and finally a chorus of voices coming to me through the centuries. A gentle word from Mr. Pepys ... a hearty chuckle from Dr. Johnson ... a sly remark from Monsieur Molière ... a rousing cry from Mr. Dickens ... and at last, at last my beloved Mr. Shakespeare, sighing into my ear, "I had rather than forty shillings I had my Book of Songs and Sonnets here." Then I knew, of course. It was clear to me what I must do. No condominium must be allowed to rise where books should dwell. *(Rises.)* I remembered the hatchet in the garage. Before Robert even missed me, I had it and was in the car and on my way. I was strong, so strong suddenly, and so happy! The library was dark, of course, and padlocks on the doors, but ... *(Pantomimes.)* ... that was nothing to me now. I smashed at the padlocks! I slashed at the doors! Oh, the strength as I lifted again and again the hatchet and brought it against the locks, into the doors, through the windows ... opening ... opening ... opening once again ... opening the doors! People came ... they tried to restrain me ... to stop me as I slashed ... and slashed ... and slashed! *At people! (She screams an almost animal cry as we see her slashing out, flailing her arms, swinging the hatchet.)*

VOICE. *(Shouts.)* Nurse! Nurse! Come quickly! *Nurse! (The Nurse rushes in, fights with Miss Penmore to restrain her.)* You'll have to give her something.

NURSE. I've got a pill right here. Now, Miss Penmore, stop this! *Stop this! (She slaps Rose across the face. Rose sinks into the chair.)* That's better. Stay there now. *(Takes pill from pocket; gets water.)* This will calm her down. Open your mouth, Miss Penmore! Rose, open your mouth! *Open it! (Rose does, swallows pill.)* Now, water. There. She'll be all right in a minute. Are you finished with her, doctor?

VOICE. Yes, I'll see her again in two weeks. Thank you, nurse. *(We hear the click of the speaker going off.)*

NURSE. All right, now you're going back to your room.

ROSE. *(Rouses slightly.)* No, please! Don't take me back there! Can't I sit here a moment? Please?

NURSE. You have to go to your room.

ROSE. Please. Just a minute.

NURSE. Well, all right. I'll go see your bed's ready. I'll be back in two minutes. *(She exits. Rose sits for a moment staring into space.)*

ROSE. Vincent? Vincent? Oh, Vincent, paint for me! Paint the most beautiful of paintings and let it burst upon the world and dazzle even the eye of God. Shall I tell our secrets? Shall I reach out my hand and lead all mankind through crassness and greed and prejudice and hate to our secret garden? I'm confined ... I'm sedated ... I despair ... I weep ... and yet I hear birds singing. You say that looking at the stars always makes you dream just as you would over black dots on a map representing villages and towns. Why shouldn't the shining dots in the sky be as reachable as the black dots on a map? As we would take a train to reach a town or village, we take death to reach a star. But could we not take life to reach a star? *(Looks upward.)* Vincent? *(The lights dim and go to black.)*

THE END

PROPERTY LIST

Glass of water (NURSE)
Pitcher of water (NURSE)
Pill (NURSE)

Abraham Lincoln Dies at Versailles

Abraham Lincoln Dies at Versailles

September, 1889

A young man of 16 sits on a wrought-iron bench reading a guidebook. He looks quite healthy, attractive and personable. One arm, however, seems to be held carefully at his side. A young girl of the same age enters, perfectly charming, carrying a lacy parasol. He looks up. She hesitates, then comes to him.

GIRL. Do you mind if I sit next to you? I'm absolutely exhausted and the next bench is miles off.
BOY. *(Politely, closes book, half rises.)* Of course.
GIRL. Thank you. *(Sits, after a moment.)* Aren't the gardens vast! And so intricately designed. I don't see how the ancients managed to rendezvous in them. I should think they'd get lost every time they set out.
BOY. Well, I expect they knew them better than we do.
GIRL. I expect. And, of course, the French can always manage to rendezvous, can't they? No matter how difficult the conditions.
BOY. So I've been told.
GIRL. Well, I've only been told. *(Boy smiles.)* What are you smiling at?
BOY. Actually, at the word "ancients." It sounds so ... archaic. As if Versailles were the pyramids.
GIRL. Well, after all, it has been over a hundred years, hasn't it? Poor Marie Antoinette! I hate sad stories, don't you?
BOY. Yes, I do.
GIRL. I refuse to believe a sad story. I simply refuse.
BOY. On so beautiful a day, it would be sacrilege.

GIRL. Exactly.

BOY. *(After a moment.)* Are you alone?

GIRL. Of course not! *(Amused.)* What are you suggesting! My mother's right over there in that bevy of English tourists. Are you?

BOY. Yes. At the moment. But I'm in France with friends.

GIRL. In France with friends. It sounds so pleasant, doesn't it?

BOY. It is.

GIRL. Older friends?

BOY. No. A couple of school chums. But they're not as interested in history as I am so we've separated for the day.

GIRL. How lucky you are not to be in a bevy of tourists! You're an American?

BOY. *(Nods.)* Could you tell by my accent?

GIRL. Instantly.

BOY. But I live in London at the moment.

GIRL. So do I! What fun! What's your name?

BOY. They call me Jack.

GIRL. What do you mean, they call you Jack?

BOY. Everybody calls me Jack. It's easier.

GIRL. Easier than what?

BOY. Oh, just ... *(Shrugs.)* ... easier than my real name.

GIRL. Why? Are you very rich?

BOY. Of course not.

GIRL. I am. We are. Very rich. They call me Susan.

BOY. How do you do?

GIRL. How do you do? Because that's my real name.

BOY. Very nice.

GIRL. My mother's an American ... I mean, she was before she married my father. So I suppose I'm half American. Why are you living in London?

BOY. Oh, well, it's because of my father's work. *(Girl looks questioningly.)* He's ...

GIRL. *(After a moment.)* He's what?

BOY. He's the American Ambassador to Great Britain.

GIRL. *(Lightly.)* I'm not impressed by that.

BOY. Well, I certainly didn't mean —

GIRL. Is that why you're so hedgy?

BOY. Hedgy?

GIRL. You hedge. Withhold. They call you Jack ... it's easier. My family, you know, moves in diplomatic circles quite easily.

BOY. I should think you'd move in any circles quite easily.

GIRL. Is that a compliment?

BOY. If you'll accept it as such.

GIRL. I should be delighted. How old are you?

BOY. I'm sixteen.

GIRL. *(Crestfallen.)* Oh.

BOY. You can't be older.

GIRL. Of course I'm not older ... but I prefer men who are.

BOY. Sorry.

GIRL. I suppose it doesn't really matter.

BOY. I don't think it matters at all.

GIRL. It depends on what we have in mind.

BOY. Well, for the moment, we might stroll.

GIRL. How can I? I'm with those awful bores! I can't just walk off with a strange man. But we could sit a bit. If we look intent in conversation I'm sure they'll think we're having a literary discussion. Or, better still, history. What is the book?

BOY. A guidebook.

GIRL. Perfect. Tell me ... I can't wait to hear ... what was the precise year of the building of the palace of Versailles?

BOY. *(Leafs through book.)* The precise year? Well, I'm not sure they say the precise year. I think it may have covered a number of years ... but to say precisely ...

GIRL. Never mind. That's quite enough. What are your secret thoughts?

BOY. I beg your pardon?

GIRL. Your secret thoughts. When you have them, what are they?

BOY. *(After a moment.)* Are you prepared for my answer?

GIRL. Aren't I?

BOY. I don't wish to shock you.

GIRL. I don't mind being shocked ... a little.

BOY. They have to do with sports.

GIRL. Sports?

BOY. To be specific — baseball.

GIRL. I'm shocked.

BOY. I warned you.

GIRL. I had hoped for something more ...

BOY. ... intellectual?

GIRL. ... unusual.

BOY. I'm afraid I'm very usual. I have no distinction whatsoever, well, except for the fact that ...

GIRL. ... except for the fact that your father is the American Ambassador to Great Britain. Oh, dear.

BOY. Except for the fact that I have an all-consuming interest in the American Civil War.

GIRL. The American Civil War? Why?

BOY. Because of my family, who played a part in it. I know every battle ... every advance ... every retreat. And what else? I'm very fond of boating and the sea, if that helps.

GIRL. Not a great deal.

BOY. I've been a frequent guest on President Arthur's yacht. Does that do anything for me?

GIRL. You see, you keep trying to impress me. Well then, do, if you feel you must. What else?

BOY. Nothing. Nothing at all. I would like it very much if you would like me for myself alone. I'm really very glad you sat down here. I was feeling quite sorry for myself and somewhat lonely and you came along and now I feel as if my entire stay in France is suddenly a success.

GIRL. That's much better ... Jack.

BOY. *(Smiles.)* Susan. *(They are silent for a moment.)*

GIRL. They'll come and take me away in a moment.

BOY. Could we have supper?

GIRL. Who? You and I?

BOY. Yes.

GIRL. The two of us? Unescorted?

BOY. Of course not. With anybody ... I suppose my friends wouldn't do, but anybody you like ... your mother ...

GIRL. She wouldn't let me. She wouldn't come. Not with a stranger ... even if your father *is* the American Ambassador. Although she's a great snob ... I mean, I love her dearly, she's a lovely person ... but a simply great snob, which amuses my father enormously considering that she comes from America ... oh, I didn't mean ...

BOY. I don't mind what you mean. Susan, we must manage somehow to have supper together!

GIRL. Yes! What shall we do?

BOY. We'll have to convince her somehow that — *(In his excitement, he drops the book. He instinctively reaches down to pick it up with his arm and winces in pain. He retrieves it with the other hand.)*

GIRL. What's wrong with your arm?

BOY. It's nothing.

GIRL. You're not in pain, are you?

BOY. It's nothing, really.

GIRL. How could you play baseball?

BOY. It happened here ... just recently ... in Paris. It's a kind of blood poisoning, apparently. It isn't serious. Please forget about it.

GIRL. Have you been to a doctor?

BOY. Yes.

GIRL. What did he say?

BOY. He said I'd live. At least, I think that's what he said. My French is a bit shaky. Please forget it. *(Susan's mother appears. She is a woman of 39 — quite old to them — richly dressed and with pretensions, but she is perfectly nice.)*

MOTHER. Susan?

GIRL. Oh, yes, mother.

MOTHER. We're walking on, Susan.

GIRL. Yes, oh, mother ... this is ... this is Jack. *(The boy and girl have both risen. Jack half bows, nervously.)*

MOTHER. How do you do? We're walking on, Susan.

BOY. *(A step forward.)* How do you do? I know this must sound impertinent on such short acquaintance, but I should like it very much if you and your daughter would take supper with me tonight.

MOTHER. I don't understand. Susan, do you know this young man?

GIRL. Well, we've only just met, but he seems awfully nice

and it would be such fun to —

MOTHER. *(To Boy.)* I'm sorry. We have plans for this evening. Come along, Susan.

BOY. *(Desperate, another step.)* I should be *very* honored if you could ... could change your plans and take supper with me as my guests at ... at a restaurant of your own choosing, Of course ...

GIRL. *(To Mother, as ammunition.)* A restaurant of our own choosing!

BOY. Susan is really such a charming person and ... while I fully understand that your natural and very right British reserve might give you pause, I do hope —

MOTHER. I am an American ... married to an Englishman ... but an American.

BOY. I'm an American, too.

GIRL. He's an American, too.

MOTHER. Versailles is over-run with Americans of a touristic nature and I hope you will not take it personally when I say there is not a one I should care to claim kinship to. *(Indicates they will leave.)* Susan.

GIRL. He hasn't told you. His father is the American Ambassador to —

BOY. No, Susan! I'll do better than that! *(To Mother.)* I don't mean to boast, but I should like to tell you my real name. Jack is merely a nickname.

MOTHER. Well?

BOY. My name is Abraham Lincoln.

MOTHER. *(Shocked.)* That is a monstrous joke!

BOY. Nevertheless, I was named after my grandfather and I am, therefore, Abraham Lincoln. My father is Robert Todd Lincoln.

MOTHER. Abraham Lincoln!

BOY. I don't generally announce it like that. It's something of a burden, really ... and certainly more than I can live up to ... but I am very proud of it and proud of my grandfather.

MOTHER. I had heard ... of course, now that I think of it ... the grandson ... but what a shock it is to meet a young man who has the right to that extraordinary name. *(Quite stunned.)* I will sit a moment. *(Sits, near tears, fumbles in purse.)* Susan, have you a handkerchief?

GIRL. *(Hands her one.)* What is it, Mother?

MOTHER. I need a moment. I'll be quite all right. But, you see, young man ... *(Reaches up, takes his hand.)* ... at one time in my life ... many years ago ... for the briefest of moments ... I ... I was privileged to be in the presence of your grandfather.

GIRL. You never told me that!

BOY. I'd love to hear about it ... anything about my grandfather.

MOTHER. Well, I was still quite a young girl ... hardly the age of Susan here, I should think ... and I was in love with President Lincoln. Oh, we all were, all the girls in that Pennsylvania farm country where we lived. For, you see, we'd seen such suffering in the war ... so close ... so near ... death seemed to be all around us ... and it was President Lincoln who'd brought us through. He was the strong fatherly figure of comfort and security ... and so we girls were in love with him. But not quite ... not quite as one would love a father ... because I will confess we had ... at least, I had ... dreams of a somewhat sensual nature regarding him. The eyes. *(To Boy.)* You must forgive me.

BOY. I forgive you.

MOTHER. At any rate, when we heard the news ... and it spread like wildfire over the Pennsylvania countryside ... the news that the president would actually come and speak at the battlefield at Gettysburg ... scarcely an hour's drive away ... well, I didn't give my father a moment's peace until he'd promised to hitch up old Dan and take me into town. And that morning, I remember, I rushed out into the fields and I picked whatever bouquet I could ... just flowers that grew wild along the fences ... and I put on my best frock ... quite plain, but clean ... and brushed my hair for an hour ... and off we went. And as we drove in, I recall my father remarking that the flowers would be wilted and, anyway, I wouldn't be able to get near the president to give them to him. And I looked at the flowers and I prayed ... I prayed all the way into

Gettysburg ... I prayed to God not to let my flowers wilt. And when we got there ... I had never heard such noise ... such excitement ... so many people slopping through the mud ... soldiers and rifles and flags and a parade and a band. I can remember it all so clearly ... and here we are at Versailles.

BOY. And you saw him?

MOTHER. Oh, of course. Immediately. He was so tall, you see, he towered over everyone else. And my heart leaped at the sight of him. But there were so many people, crowding and shoving ... and we had to stand when the speeches began ... it was all outdoors and no chairs ... not for the likes of us ... and so we stood ankle-deep in the mud at the rear of the crowd trying to catch an occasional glimpse of the dignitaries on the platform. And one of them droned on and on and on and I looked with absolute heartache at my flowers as they wilted and wilted and wilted. And then finally President Lincoln began his speech and I thought, oh, dear Lord, let it be short ... let it be short ... and it was and a grave disappointment ... some people had come so far, you see, and he'd really only said a few words and I remember there was a kind of rumble of discontent over the crowd as he finished. They couldn't quite believe it. And in that moment I darted ... I positively darted away from my father ... into the crowd ... through legs and under elbows ... I was quite small ... and before anyone could stop me I was actually standing on the platform and looking up at the gigantic form of the president. And I said, twice, I remember, "President Lincoln, please! President Lincoln, please!" and somebody started to pull me away, but the president stopped them and I held up my wilted flowers and I said, "Here!" Well, he bent over to take the poor things, but someone snatched them out of my hand ... I suppose they were certainly not considered worthy of the president ... and that would have been the end of it except that an extraordinary thing happened. He was wearing ... he was wearing one of those ridiculous stovepipe hats, you know, that men wore in those days ... and in bending over, it fell off his head. Right off his head. So he had to bend over still further to retrieve it and as he did so his remarkable head was for a moment on a level with my own ... and I looked into his eyes ... and he smiled ... and he suddenly kissed me ... *(Indicates forehead.)* ... here ... exactly here ... and then he was gone. But that kiss ... his kiss ... I have carried with me all my life ... exactly here. *(Sighs, rises.)* Well, I'm sure there is nothing more boring to young people than to hear —

BOY. Oh, no, thank you. He seemed so alive for a moment. I never knew him, of course, or my grandmother. She died the year before I was born. But I've read everything about him I can get my hands on and I'm trying sincerely to be as much like him as I can.

MOTHER. You have the name. That in itself is a great gift. And you must carry it on.

GIRL. Isn't he the president who brought about the purchase of Louisiana?

MOTHER. No, he is not. Shame on you, Susan. *(To Boy.)* They learn nothing of American history in England except that they were revolutionaries. We shall be delighted to take supper with you this evening, Mr. Lincoln.

GIRL. *(Delighted.)* Oh, Mother!

BOY. That is wonderful of you!

MOTHER. But, Susan, look! We must catch up with the others.

GIRL. Yes, Mother, but can't we ... *(Moves closer to Boy.)* ... walk a little behind? We'll follow.

MOTHER. Of course, you may. *(Hesitates, to Boy.)* Before I forget ... if you will permit the liberty ... there is something I should like to give you ... *(Indicates his forehead.)* ... exactly here ... *(Kisses him, looks into his eyes.)* ... from your grandfather.

BOY. Thank you.

MOTHER. Don't get too far behind, Susan.

GIRL. We won't, Mother. *(Mother exits.)* You see? Everything worked out perfectly!

BOY. Perfectly!

GIRL. I always expect life to work out perfectly ... and it does. Shall I take your arm?

BOY. I'd be honored. *(Girl almost takes the wrong arm, switches.)*

GIRL. This arm. *(They start walking.)* I'm so glad the doctor said you're going to live. I think people *should* live … especially people like you who have everything to live for … *(They are gone.)*

THE END

PROPERTY LIST

Lacy parasol (GIRL)
Guide book (BOY)

Elephants

Elephants

Rome, 108 A.D.

A young man in a toga of expensive cut lies on the ground in a drunken stupor, a jug hanging limply from his hand. He is asleep, but stirs slightly and uneasily, as if dreaming. His name is Arcadius. We hear the call of "Arcadius! Arcadius!" and then a second young man appears. He is perhaps a little rougher in manner than his friend, but they are both of the upper classes. His name is Domitian. He hurries forward when he sees Arcadius, which is, by the way, pronounced with the last syllable as "oos." He bends down.

DOMITIAN. Arcadius! Arcadius, wake up! It's me — Domitian. *(Shakes Arcadius.)* Arcadius, what's wrong with you? *(Arcadius opens his eyes ever so slightly.)*

ARCADIUS. Go away!

DOMITIAN. *(Picks up jug, turns it over; empty.)* You're drunk!

ARCADIUS. Yes.

DOMITIAN. You don't drink.

ARCADIUS. I'm drunk. Go away, Domitian.

DOMITIAN. What happened? Did she refuse you?

ARCADIUS. *(A flicker of interest.)* Who?

DOMITIAN. Marciana.

ARCADIUS. I had forgotten.

DOMITIAN. Did you ask her?

ARCADIUS. What?

DOMITIAN. Will she marry you?

ARCADIUS. I had forgotten her.

DOMITIAN. *(Tries to pick Arcadius up.)* Come! I'll take you home.

ARCADIUS. *(Resists.)* No.

DOMITIAN. There's sewage. It's an alley. You can't lie here. *(He attempts to pull Arcadius up again.)*

ARCADIUS. No.

DOMITIAN. Your parents are frantic. Do you know you've been gone for over a week?

ARCADIUS. I know that.

DOMITIAN. We've searched for you ... the entire household ... we've searched all of Rome ... except the worst part ... except here. Come home.

ARCADIUS. I can't.

DOMITIAN. What's happened?

ARCADIUS. I want more wine.

DOMITIAN. There isn't any. And if there were, I'd drink it myself.

ARCADIUS. Get me more wine, Domitian.

DOMITIAN. No. You're going home. *(He attempts to pull Arcadius up again, but Arcadius wrenches himself loose, staggers to his feet, moves slightly away.)*

ARCADIUS. I'm never going home! I'm never going to see them again ever! My family! My friends! I'm going to curl up ... *(He does.)* ... here ... in the sewage ... in the cool and comforting trickle of sewage ... so that when I die I shall be washed away into the sewers of Rome.

DOMITIAN. *(Pulls Arcadius up again.)* You're not going to die and you're not going to lie in the sewage!

ARCADIUS. *(Lashes out.)* Get away! You fiend! You demon!

DOMITIAN. Arcadius, stop this! I'm your friend. We've known each other since we were little boys.

ARCADIUS. *(Relenting.)* I know ... I know. I'm sorry, Domitian. It's just ... it's just that I'm so frightened.

DOMITIAN. Of what?

ARCADIUS. Of what? Of everything. Of every shadow ... every leaf ... every fluttering wing ... every bark of a dog ... of clouds that cross the moon ... and the glare of the sun ... and the slightest breeze ... and the sound of rain ... and any eye that dares, however innocently, to look into mine ... or a cough in the night ... and even ... even ... the most terrifying of all ... the beating of my own heart.

DOMITIAN. That's nonsense. You're the bravest of us all. When the cottage of your slaves caught fire, you alone rushed

in ... you saved lives at the risk of your own ...
ARCADIUS. Did I? It seems impossible.
DOMITIAN. Come.
ARCADIUS. *(Firmly.)* I will not go home!
DOMITIAN. All right ... *(Takes arm.)* ... but come away from this sewage. The smell alone! Come and sit here and tell me what's happened to you.
ARCADIUS. *(Moving with him.)* The most terrible of all things, Domitian. The most frightening of all things. *(They sit.)* Give me your hand, dear friend. We are Roman gentlemen, are we not? Gently born ... the keepers of slaves gently treated ... of sisters gently nurtured ... above the rabble ... aware of the savagery that rages around us, but sheltered by soft music and peaceful gardens behind walls a century old.
DOMITIAN. We are.
ARCADIUS. *(Nods.)* Do you go to the games, Domitian? Have you been to the circuses?
DOMITIAN. Yes ... once or twice.
ARCADIUS. Have you? Did you ... enjoy them?
DOMITIAN. Yes ... the races.
ARCADIUS. Nothing else?
DOMITIAN. The combat, if they're fairly matched.
ARCADIUS. Nothing else?
DOMITIAN. Nothing else.
ARCADIUS. Until eight days ago, I had never been to such an event. I like to think of myself as a poet ... in the manner of the Greek poets. My father laughs at me, but I write ... I scribble ... I try to make sense of the stars and the moon and the waves of the sea. I attempt to illuminate beauty. But no more. Not now.
DOMITIAN. Why not?
ARCADIUS. Because of the worst of luck ... a chance encounter with the Emperor. Marciana is a great favorite of the Empress, you know, and so she had been asked to spend a week with her at her villa. A great honor. And she in turn asked me to escort her there. Well, I've been so enamored of her ... the slightest whim ... and so I went. But as we approached, the gates were flung open and out came the Em-

peror in full regalia on his way into the city with his entourage. We stepped aside, of course, but he saw us. It's said he once loved my mother, you know. And he said, "Ah, Arcadius, we will see you tomorrow at the games." Well, I couldn't say, "No, you won't." He would have had me killed on the spot.

DOMITIAN. Yes.

ARCADIUS. And so I bowed and nodded. And I had no alternative. You know how he scans the crowd ... how he has notes taken of who has come to his games and who hasn't.

DOMITIAN. And punishes them.

ARCADIUS. Yes. I had to go, if only to be seen ... if only to stay alive.

DOMITIAN. Of course.

ARCADIUS. I wish I had said no and let him kill me then and there.

DOMITIAN. The games offended you? The senseless shedding of blood?

ARCADIUS. Not at first. Gladiators seem to me to be bred for that purpose. Let them hack away at one another. Even let a dwarf duel with a prostitute to the death. I was sickened, but I wasn't overcome by nausea. And then ...

DOMITIAN. Was it animals?

ARCADIUS. Yes. Elephants. People were marched into the arena ... not marched ... pulled, dragged ... and they were forced to lie down on their backs in the dirt and they were strapped with their arms out and their legs out ... strapped to stakes ... flat on the ground ... looking up at the sky. It occurred to me ... and I hope it's true ... that they were blinded by the sun. And then a great cheer went up and I saw that elephants were being led into the arena. I suddenly became dizzy. I stood up with the crowd and I could hardly keep my balance. I felt a rising hysteria within me and I tried desperately to hold onto my reason ... to tell myself that whatever happened it was good ... that it was how the Emperor kept the people entertained and submissive. But that was instantly crowded out of my mind by the sight I saw before me. The elephants were prodded forward by spears and, if need be, torches. They resisted ... what delicate and sensitive creatures they appeared to be beside their keepers ... and despite their great size. They loathed what they were being forced to do. And then I saw a tall handsome man and woman ... blond ... blue-eyed ...

DOMITIAN. From the north.

ARCADIUS. From the north. And with them was a small child of no more than five or six that the man held in his arms ... a little girl with golden hair. Then she was wrenched away from him and they screamed ... the parents screamed and fought wildly to save their child, but they were staked down on the dirt. And a small doll-like object that the little girl clutched ... made of nothing but rags ... was pulled from her tiny hands and, with much laughter from the crowd, flung into the air. And the child was staked down ... and then ... and then ... the elephants advanced ... prodded, burned ... until they had stepped on first the father ... and then the mother ... and then ... at the exact moment the giant foot of an elephant came down to crush that lovely child ... oh, Domitian!

DOMITIAN. *(Holds him.)* Don't, Arcadius!

ARCADIUS. At that exact moment ... she turned her head and I swear that the eyes of that exquisite child met mine ... and I saw in them the most horrible of all things. I saw the agony of innocence ... the uncomprehending horror at the moment of evil's triumph. And the huge animal was made to bring down his full weight on her small sweet form ... and I heard ... suddenly I heard, Domitian ... I heard a ghastly sound within my head ... and the sun suddenly beat into my brain with terrifying violence ... and there was a rush of great wings ... and I cried out because I knew ... I knew what had flown from my body. I knew, Domitian, that in that moment I had lost my soul.

DOMITIAN. It was the sight of blood ... the heat ... the crowd ...

ARCADIUS. No. I had lost my soul.

DOMITIAN. She was only a slave ... or perhaps a Christian ...

ARCADIUS. She was a child ... an innocent child. What

could she know of slavery or Christianity?

DOMITIAN. And what do you know of souls?

ARCADIUS. What?

DOMITIAN. Are you in league with the gods? Do you know what a soul is?

ARCADIUS. No. I only know I've lost mine.

DOMITIAN. Arcadius, listen to me. You must forget this. You must let me take you home. You must go on with your life. Whatever happened, it's all behind you now. After all, it's been eight days since you went to the arena.

ARCADIUS. Oh, no.

DOMITIAN. What?

ARCADIUS. I've been there every day. I'm there from early dawn until late at night when I buy my jug of wine and drink until dawn again. I go to watch the elephants. I cheer with the crowd. I throw flowers into the arena at the sight of blood. I laugh at torture. I applaud pain. I give a standing ovation to death.

DOMITIAN. But why?

ARCADIUS. I told you. I've lost my soul. *(Domitian stares at him a moment, then back slowly away as the lights dim and the curtain falls.)*

THE END

PROPERTY LIST

Jug (ARCADIUS)

Requiem for Us

~~no subjs~~

/ Middle-aged couple await end of time

/ 1m 1w

Requiem for Us

Time: The future.

As the curtain rises a middle-aged couple sit together. They wear formal evening clothes and are quite sophisticated in the manner of a Coward comedy.

There is no set. They are perched upon ornately designed iron chairs, the kind that might be found on the terrace of an elegant estate.

SHE. What time is it?
HE. *(Looks at watch.)* Three fifty-four.
SHE. Six minutes.
HE. Yes.
SHE. Shall we talk or…?
HE. Whatever you like.
SHE. I don't know. It seems so … odd.
HE. Yes.
SHE. I've never died before.
HE. *(Laughs.)* Well, I guess none of us …
SHE. I can't quite believe it.
HE. I do wish it weren't so.
SHE. At least, lovely, isn't it? To have warning? A little time?
HE. I hope so.
SHE. To savor it. To remember.
HE. Yes.
SHE. Such a strange feeling. No future. One's always had a future, hasn't one? Planning. What to do? Tomorrow. The next day.
HE. Death is a future.
SHE. *(Laughs.)* You can't possibly know that.
HE. I believe it. Somehow.

SHE. Are you religious?
HE. No. Are you?
SHE. Yes. But I don't believe it.
HE. Well …
SHE. We could sit quietly, I suppose, with our hands folded. But doesn't that seem stupidly resigned? Like sheep?
HE. We can do whatever we want, I should think. I don't see why not.
SHE. Actually, we ought to be fighting it. We ought to be angry … clawing.
HE. No good. No time.
SHE. Six minutes.
HE. Less. *(Pause.)*
SHE. The animals. Why is it I feel sorriest for the animals?
HE. Do you?
SHE. Yes, rather. It's like a forest fire. Not of their doing and yet they're trapped … helpless … dying. Burning to death, those who have never lit a fire.
HE. *(Shrugs.)* Well, if it's justice you're after …
SHE. No, I'm not after anything.
HE. I don't think you should look for justice.
SHE. No. *(Pause.)*
HE. Would you like it if I put my arm around you?
SHE. Not especially. I'm sorry. I don't need that and I don't want that.
HE. I only meant to —
SHE. You only meant to comfort yourself by putting your arm around me.
HE. Are we going to argue in these last few minutes?
SHE. I don't think it matters what we do. *(Pause.)*
HE. What I should really like to do …
SHE. Yes?
HE. I should like to make an old person laugh.
SHE. What?
HE. I should like to make an old person laugh.
SHE. I heard you, but why?
HE. Well, it smacks to me of courage.
SHE. Does it?

HE. Yes, you see, in the face of the grave ... laughter.

SHE. I do see. *(Pause.)* What else?

HE. I should like to see the sun shining upon the side of a stark white building that has only a single tiny window near the roof. Blazing white light against one small darkened space behind which ...

SHE. Behind which?

HE. Behind which is all of humanity.

SHE. Oh?

HE. In the form of a solitary scrubwoman.

SHE. Ah!

HE. She cleans.

SHE. Of course. *(Pause.)* How much more time?

HE. A few minutes.

SHE. A very few. *(Thinks.)* I should like ...

HE. Yes?

SHE. I should like to walk along the shore ... a sandy beach ... miles and miles of it ... and suddenly I come upon —

HE. What?

SHE. The tiniest of turtles.

HE. Really?

SHE. Yes, the tiniest of turtles. Making his way ... making his way across what must, to him, be infinite space. I should like to pick him up and say to him ...

HE. What in the world would you say?

SHE. I would say this: "You will get there. You will reach it ... and once you do it will be worth it. But not ... not because you are there ... but because you made the journey."

HE. Ah! *(Pause.)* Would it help if I said I loved you?

SHE. I don't see why it should.

HE. No. You may be wiser than I.

SHE. But it might help if ...

HE. Yes?

SHE. Would you rise?

HE. Surely. *(He does.)*

SHE. Would you raise your fist? *(He does.)*

HE. Yes. And?

SHE. I don't really know.

HE. I do. *(Looks up defiantly.)* I will say that out of the night and the darkness as we move among the stars and all of life dances in this monstrous and magical void, I will be heard and I will caress with my hand the storms of the universe. And I will leave in the depths of eternity a sigh ... a sweet and tender sigh that will float for ever and ever in the winds of the worlds of which we know and of which we will never know. And you will remember me ... and you will remember me ... *(He sits and looks at her.)*

SHE. I should like to leave a single jewel ... a shining bauble that will glitter just a little as it sinks into the ever-widening sea. The merest flicker of light in the darkness that one can see from a great, great distance. And one will ask, "What is that?" And perhaps one will stretch one's arm into the depths of eternity and come to rest upon it and exclaim, "Isn't it lovely!"

HE. Yes.

SHE. And shall I leave ... shall I leave a strain of music? To remind them.

HE. Yes.

SHE. And shall I leave a printed word? To remind them.

HE. Yes.

SHE. And shall I leave a dash of color? Just to remind them. Just to prove that it was so?

HE. Yes.

SHE. What is the time?

HE. Four o'clock.

SHE. Well, then ...

HE. Goodbye.

SHE. Goodbye. *(The lights darken and the curtain falls.)*

THE END

PROPERTY LIST

Wrist watch (HE)

NEW
PLAYS

THE AFRICAN COMPANY PRESENTS
RICHARD III
by Carlyle Brown

EDWARD ALBEE'S
FRAGMENTS and THE MARRIAGE PLAY

IMAGINARY LIFE
by Peter Parnell

MIXED EMOTIONS
by Richard Baer

THE SWAN
by Elizabeth Egloff

Write for information as to availability

DRAMATISTS PLAY SERVICE, Inc.
440 Park Avenue South New York, N.Y. 10016

NEW PLAYS

THE LIGHTS
by Howard Korder

THE TRIUMPH OF LOVE
by James Magruder

LATER LIFE
by A.R. Gurney

THE LOMAN FAMILY PICNIC
by Donald Margulies

A PERFECT GANESH
by Terrence McNally

SPAIN
by Romulus Linney

Write for information as to availability